Inside Out

Published by Accent Press Ltd – 2009

ISBN 9781906373757

The Quick Reads project in Wales is a joint venture between Basic
Skills Cymru and the Welsh Books Council. Titles are funded through
Basic Skills Cymru as part of the National Basic Skills Strategy for
Wales on behalf of the Welsh Assembly Government.

Printed and bound in the UK

Cover design by Red Dot Design

CYNGOR LLYFRAU CYMRU
WELSH BOOKS COUNCIL

Noddir gan
Lywodraeth Cynulliad Cymru
Sponsored by
Welsh Assembly Government

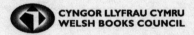

Sgiliau Sylfaenol Cymru
Basic Skills

Inside Out

Real life stories
from Parc Prison, Bridgend

ACCENT PRESS LTD

Contents

Let My Dream Come True

David

I'm stuck here within these walls.

Peaceful but stressed. Waiting for my case to commence, listening for that dreaded word 'guilty' or the thrilling sound of 'not guilty'.

Why does this place seem to make dreams vanish?

The truth is we need hope and that's where God can help us.

As summer passes and autumn appears, the leaves gather on the yard, the birds fly south and darkness comes more quickly. But don't worry, the end is near, your freedom will soon be here.

What will you do?

If you have a dream, why not let it come true?

Where am I?

Not in a good place, as you can see.

This is not my first sentence but it's most definitely my last.

Let me take you back to before I started offending.

From as young as I can remember life wasn't easy.

My mother has been in and out of prison since I was five or six years of age. She was constantly offending, doing stuff such as shoplifting to feed her heroin addiction, which has left me scared inside. And my father is an alcoholic.

I do have a brother who is sensible and supporting, although he hasn't always been. When he was sixteen he spent a short time in prison. Then he got out and went to college, now he's now a fully qualified fabricating welder and studying to be a financial adviser.

He has inspired me a great deal and proves that just because you've been to prison it doesn't mean you can't change.

So remember that.

In junior school I was like any other kid. I loved school, sport, cartoons, being with my friends, climbing trees, playing with my Action Men. On occasions I even wet the bed.

I wasn't thick or dull; I was a bright boy. I did well in my exams and the teachers loved me. I was the perfect student.

Me and my uncle Jeff, we were very close.

He was my best mate, well, second best. My teddy Harry the Hippo was first.

Jeff taught me the alphabet, to count and to tie my shoelaces. He used to take me with him to visit his friends Janey and Tegs. I used to play on the computer most of the time and they would be in the kitchen smoking a bong. Then they would want to join me playing on Tekkon.

"Winner stays on."

"Ha stoners."

Not one of them could get me off.

That may not seem like fun to you. Maybe you and your family go on holiday or to the cinema together. Na, not me, and that's just the way it was. I loved it. I wouldn't have changed it even if I could.

This one time I slept up at my nan's. I remember it like it was yesterday. Nan cooking, me and my cousin trying to wrestle with my granddad. We used to wind him up by saying "dddddd fat man" – it drove him mad. If he was getting the better of us my nan would attack him with the remote. She was our back-up plan.

One night my uncle Jeff came home. He was a great believer in God and Jesus Christ, he truly was, and I'd never seen him so happy. He was dancing, singing and chasing me and my cousin around. It was wild.

That night we all went to sleep at Nan's.

When I woke up the next morning before I got ready to go home I asked Nan if I could say good-bye to Jeff.

She replied, "No. He's sleeping."

I didn't think too much about it. But later that day I found out that Jeff had died in his sleep.

I believe he knew it was going to happen.

What if I had gone to say goodbye and he'd been still alive? That plays with my mind sometimes.

I was ten when he passed away. I will never forget him.

As time went on life didn't change much.

Mum was still locked up. My brother Karl had moved into a flat. It was just me and Dad. But if needed Nan helped out.

When I started high school things were looking good. I was doing well in education and found I was talented at sport. I took that talent outside of school and started boxing.

I soon picked up the main steps and

became quite skilled. My dad was proud of me and I was proud of myself.

After about three months I started having bouts, and after six months I became Welsh Champion and felt over the moon.

But school started getting hard and I began fighting and smoking cannabis and lost my interest in boxing. I got expelled from school when I was young, and I was only fifteen when I started drinking and taking ecstasy, which led to a life of crime. I was fighting, shoplifting and robbing cars. After about a year of drugs and crime I started an 'include' course' and sat the exams and had the highest results since the course had started. But not even that could stop me being a criminal.

In 2007 I received a jail sentence for wounding with intent, which made me think about life a lot. But when I got out I started drinking again, and I used to go into town and sniff coke and enjoy myself.

I also got back into boxing and was told if I won the Welsh Championships again I might be allowed to enter the Olympics. That is still my dream.

I also started a sports coaching

development course, coaching boxing and five-a-side football tournaments to young teenagers from the Youth Offending Team who had just started getting into crime.

Maybe I could show them what I have been through, maybe I could be an example to them, to encourage them to turn their lives around, and that would make me proud.

I find myself here again, where I have found God and how to be me. But all of my dreams are still there and I'm planning to fulfil them for myself and my family.

So, no matter what has happened to you, if you have a dream try to make it come true.

The Hole

Duane

I've got one small bed and one small sink, one small toilet and a small TV.

The window has bars, a reminder that I can't go anywhere. It's cold in here, but warm outside. I'm constantly in the shade. Where am I? I'm in a mess, a nightmare, I'm in a hole, I'm a nobody, I'm an invisible island, my temperature fluctuates from boiling-kettle heat to ice-cube cold, the frustrated sea pounds the sand, dark clouds hover and the rains fall. I'm marooned.

My mum and dad have become letters; I'm going crazy waiting for them to be washed on to the shore or to slide under the door.

I was six years old and I was insecure and terrified. Mum and Dad had split up. My world collapsed like an old wooden bridge and my heart felt like a crushed can getting kicked around the kerbs of a council estate; it sounded hollow and dead.

The four of us had to move to London and live in a refuge. We were my mum, who had a dream to become a fashion designer, my older sister, me and my younger sister Claire. Mum was always struggling, we had no money and us kids were naughty, especially me.

Memories of Marks and Spencer's food still stay with me. Once a week the refuge received parcels of close-to-gone-off food, ready meals, sandwiches, prawns and pink and white coconut cakes. I guess that would have tasted like heaven to people in some parts of the world, but it put me off eating food with the sell-by date gone.

When my Mum cooked it would always be the same kind of food: tuna pasta bakes, chicken, peas and rice and it would all take ages to be ready. I felt so hungry that my tummy would growl, as I looked in the full oven at the cooked chicken and all four rings on the hob being used to boil rice and vegetables.

I can still hear Mum say to me, "Eat them all up and you will be big and strong."

I was impatient. "How long left, Mum?"

"Ten minutes, Duane."

Even at that age I knew it would be longer.

"Mum, I'm starving."

"You're not starving, you're hungry."

I loved that moment when dinner was ready and we were given our food. The smell, my taste buds on edge and my mouth watering. It kinda reminds me of prison, of waiting to be released.

It was hard living in the Refuge.

Mum and I always seemed to be moving, and I missed my dad. Me and Dad were close. Don't get me wrong, me and Mum were close too and I loved them equally, but I loved them in different ways. Dad was my male role-model.

I would have liked a brother, but some things aren't meant to be.

Dad did a little stretch a while back and he was sent far away to Laverne. Sometimes I used to go and visit him. Mum would take me with my grampy, Dad's father. We would travel to Cardiff and Swansea prison and eat donuts and chocolates on the train. That cheered me up. What made me feel really good was when Dad had a home leave from prison. We would go to sign on together in Llanedeyrn Police Station. And we'd go swimming and bike riding together.

The best times of all, though, were when Dad used to blow up balloons, then send them down the river and I was allowed to fire at them with a rifle. Dad didn't ever kill animals. He always said to only kill an animal if you were going to eat it. He was good like that.

When I used to walk along the bank of the Rumney river with my dad, who was my king, I couldn't stop talking.

"Are we there yet, Dad?"

"No, not yet, Champ."

He always called me that. I liked it, and it made me feel secure.

I always knew when we were near 'cos that's when he pulled out of his pocket the packet of balloons.

"We're nearly there, Champ."

I would feel the butterflies in my tummy flutter faster and faster.

"YESSS," I would say, clenching my fists together.

"We're here, Champ."

Dad would get the air rifle out of the case. He would have already blown up at least three balloons.

"Can I have first shot, Dad, please?"

"Yes."

He loaded the pellet into the barrel. Clunk, click, the gun was loaded and the safety on.

"Ready?" he would say as he threw the balloon into the water.

"Quick. Let's go, Champ."

We would run down the river and at a certain point stop. Dad would take the safety clip off the gun, he would drop to his knees, hold me and we would both aim and shoot. BANG! The pellet would fly out into the balloon, tearing it to shreds.

I loved guns. I used to play with green plastic soldiers and green tanks when I was small. I watched war movies and gangster films. I wanted to grow up and be a gangster and have a gun of my own.

My mum was amazing – she could perform miracles. Even though we lived in the Refuge she managed to get us housed in north London. She was a magician with money, she could budget really well and she had a big surprise waiting for us.

Sadly it wasn't my mum who told us what the surprise was, it was my nan.

"Duane, Claire, come here."

"OK, Nan." I knew it was something good.

"Don't tell your mum, but she's taking you to the Caribbean for four weeks."

We were going to Antigua to visit our family. Mum was upset with Nan; she thought she had spoilt the surprise. Nan just couldn't keep a secret.

This was magic.

When Sharon and I heard the news we were buzzing like two bumble bees flying around a mountain of honey.

The relationship I had with my grampy, Dad's father, was good.

He did some naughty things, though.

When we went to Roath Park to feed the ducks, Grampy would put mustard on the bread and when the ducks ate it they would make a noise, shake their heads and go under the water, acting really weird.

Sometimes he used to take me to Asda. We'd walk around and he'd tell me to pinch something to eat like cooked chicken, crab sticks and prawns, and we'd eat them in between the aisles.

When I was about twelve I used to ask my grampy to take me down to Bute Town to see the prostitutes. I liked seeing the women in their short skirts and red lipstick.

After feeding the ducks and if it was dark I

would say, "Come on, Gramps, let's go and see the prostitutes." And he would take me.

Growing up, I was confused.

I was smoking weed and couldn't afford it, so I'd rob people to pay for it. Dad didn't want me to get into trouble and thought he was helping me when he started giving me enough weed to sell and earn enough money to buy my own.

This conflicted with Mum's advice, which was: "Don't forget, Duane, you're somebody. Live clean, wash every day and live smart."

Well, here I am in prison. But where am I?

Prison is not helping me find out.

I do know I want to keep my head down. The memory of being in this hole and feeling anonymous will stay with me.

I want to lead a normal life, I wanna break the chain.

I miss my mum and dad.

No matter how many letters I receive, I'll always be waiting for more.

Tiger Bay

Nathan

My mum was born in the Valleys. My dad is Indian and was born in Malaysia.

Mum came to Tiger Bay to work in a dental surgery. Dad was a seaman and docked in Cardiff. When Dad went to get his teeth checked out he met Mum and started to chat her up. They fell in love, got married and had three children.

When I started my first year in high school I was doing well at subjects like physical education and geography. My favourite subject was PE. I was very excited going to school and learning new things.

But somewhere along the line something went wrong. Me. I started to miss the lessons I hated and then began to smoke cannabis with my mates. I enjoyed doing that, but the problem was my head was all over the place and I started to get paranoid. Me and my friends used to skip school and go to

Llanrumney Fields. I used to feel safe with them there but my paranoia made me think that the teachers were watching my every move.

And every time I smoked cannabis, I was on the munchies – I was really hungry.

One day my mates and I all went to our local chippy. On the way out we passed a bunch of girls eating their chip butties and one of the girls started whistling. I shouted over my shoulder, "Who are you whistling at?"

She said, "You."

I began to feel shy. She was very attractive with blonde hair and lovely blue eyes. I didn't know what to say to her so she gave me her mobile number and said she'd give me a call later.

I said my goodbyes and carried on walking; I hadn't got very far when she shouted out for my number.

After I arrived home and had chilled for a few hours I thought I would phone her, but before I could pick up the phone it rang and a voice said, "Hello. It's Sherelle. I forgot to tell you my name." She already knew mine – she'd asked one of my mates.

We arranged to meet on Llanrumney Bridge. I was really nervous waiting for her. She took me to her house where I met her dad. He had no legs and was in a wheelchair. I was pretty scared meeting him, but he seemed a very nice man. I guess he knew I was frightened.

I was still smoking cannabis when I was with Sherelle and she started smoking it too. I knew things were going wrong – it was a bad mistake, her smoking too. I didn't want her to smoke and end up like me missing out on my education. I told her not to smoke, but really I couldn't tell her what to do with her life

When I left high school we were still in a relationship together. By then I'd given up cannabis, my head was so messed up. But Sherelle was unable to give up – she said she couldn't, it relaxed her. For my own sake I had to end the relationship. If I hadn't I would have gone back to the ganja.

I was gutted losing her; I walked out of her life feeling empty. My friends wanted to know why, so I told them but said I didn't want to talk about it any more.

During my later teenage years I started to hang around with my mates outside shops drinking a lot of alcohol. The drink made me angry; I got into a lot of trouble smashing bottles against walls and became aggressive towards people, including my mates. They used to wind me up about things and talk about my ex-girlfriend; this would make me lash out at them. But I still used to hang around with them.

Then I started to steal things. I would go shoplifting in Cardiff town centre; I started with bottles of spirits, then anything I could get my hands on because I was getting away with it.

As soon as I got caught and had a criminal record I felt so ashamed of myself. The problem was that I was now addicted to alcohol.

When my family found out they were so angry with me that they grounded me for two weeks, but I used to sneak out of the window and continued stealing to get money for drink.

Of course, I eventually got caught by a security guard in town, who threatened to call the police. I started to cry and pleaded with him, but he didn't listen to me.

I was arrested and put into a cell. The cell was dirty and very cold. I started shaking because I was freezing and needed a drink of vodka or cider or both. My head was so messed up.

I was so scared when they told me I would

have to stay in police custody overnight. They gave me a blanket to sleep on, which smelt like a dog had been lying on it. I tried getting my head down but it was impossible to sleep; I was too uncomfortable. Most of the night was spent with my head down the toilet being sick. When I did wake up I found I had fallen asleep on the filthy floor.

I needed help so I started punching the cell door, I couldn't handle being locked in in such a small place.

My solicitor warned me that I would be sent to prison. I asked him to help me, to stop the court sending me down. He didn't say anything as I was handcuffed and put into the Reliance van. I was terrified.

Imagine my surprise when I walked into court and saw my ex, Sherelle, sitting there. My solicitor had already told me that the judge was strict, so when I pleaded guilty and told him what I had done I didn't think I had much hope. But it must have been my lucky day because the judge gave me a Community Order for twelve months. I was so happy and thanked my solicitor for doing his best.

When I started to walk out of the courtroom someone tapped me on the shoulder and when I turned I had another surprise. It was Sherelle and she wanted us to get back together. I couldn't believe it.

I told her how ashamed I was of my life. She didn't care about what had happened – she said what was done was done. She also told me that she'd stopped smoking cannabis. So there we were back together again.

My life started to get better and I thanked Sherelle for being with me every step of the way. She didn't have to be there, but she was. I told her I was grateful.

My family gave me another chance, which made me so happy. I had help getting off the drink and it was hard, but I did it. If I hadn't, I would have lost a lot of loved ones. My head had been so messed up I didn't realise how many people I was hurting.

When I was sorted, I went to find a job though there didn't seem much hope of finding one, and everyone wanted someone with experience. I guess if I'd tried my best in school I would have got my qualifications and got a good job, but I failed.

Don't think I'm trying to make you feel sorry for me because I ain't. I blame myself for the things I've done in my life. I was young and didn't care about anyone else, only myself, which wasn't fair, because a lot of people were trying to keep me out of trouble. I have to thank them for that.

I don't know how it all went wrong again or why I started mixing with bad people and stealing again.

I wasn't shoplifting for alcohol. I was stealing cars and going joy-riding with my mates. I started smoking cannabis and once again couldn't see what I was doing to my family and myself.

Life was a mess, my head was a mess. When I got home in the early hours of the morning I would wake my parents because I had forgotten my key, and someone would have to get out of bed to let me in. Everyone was angry and they would start shouting at me.

I'd fall asleep with all my clothes on, wake up with a dry mouth, drink water from the tap in the bathroom, look at myself in the mirror and see someone who looked and felt like shit. I knew I needed to clean myself up.

Even when Sherelle phoned up asking where I was I would lie. I didn't want her to know I was stealing cars and joy-riding with my mates. I needed to stop but I liked the buzz of driving and staying out late at night.

There was often hardly any petrol in the cars I stole, so I would go into petrol stations with false number plates on, fill up the tank and drive off at speed. Eventually I had to get out of Cardiff because I was too well known to the police.

But I carried on stealing and making money for my cannabis. I also got back into drinking. I was robbing garages and stealing petrol lawn mowers, mountain bikes, tools and anything I could get my hands on. By stealing people's things I realise now I was robbing people of their livelihood but this never crossed my mind at the time.

Now when I think of it I'm horrified at what I was capable of doing.

With the benefit of being off drugs, and the passing of time, I do regret what I did.

I managed to get off cannabis; the problem was that I was still drinking alcohol to excess. Under the influence of drink I started fighting, got arrested and sent to prison.

Once my mind was clear I was able to consider the number of people that I must have hurt during my rampage. I'm filled with regret and wish I hadn't done it.

There are left-over problems, which I'm trying to sort out, stuff I'm trying to work on.

But after this is all over I know I will be a better person.

My Big Mistakes

Gareth

How it started: I was sitting in my boxroom bedroom, when the door opened and my stepfather walked in and beat me black and blue.

I thought this happened to everyone.

Social Services came and arrested him.

And they took me to Ty Mawr Boarding School.

The school used to take us children on trips. We went fishing, canoeing, mountain climbing, playing cricket and many other physical activities.

But when the big boys took me under their wing, I started to get into trouble.

Running away with the boys became my favourite sport. We would hang around in groups, which attracted the interest of the police. The police would have to take us back to Ty Mawr in a van. When we got back we were all punished and locked in our dormitories until they decided to let us out.

This behaviour developed into me getting drunk, sniffing glue, smoking and getting into trouble with the police.

At fifteen I was thrown out of the boarding school. I had no home, no job, no money and no prospects. I have relied on myself all of my life, I've had to.

By the time I reached seventeen, I was serving a six-month sentence in Portland Prison for burglary. When I was there I worked on the gardens. I was part of the Garden Party. But within two months of being released I was back in trouble and back inside for another six months.

When I got released this time I travelled by bus to Great Yarmouth to live with my Auntie Pat. She ran a Bed and Breakfast and gave me a job cleaning.

That's where I met Jodie, who introduced me to amphetamines and cannabis. Now I needed to feed a drug habit, which meant back to crime.

So I was arrested again and served two years in Norwich prison, where I worked in the kitchen washing trays. After a while I moved up in the world to onion peeling, and eventually I was serving the food.

When I got out Auntie Pat didn't want me back at her house. So I decided to go home to Wales with Jodie. I was now old enough to get a flat from the council and get it paid for out of benefits.

I managed to get a job on a farm plucking chickens. I remained there for two years and stayed clear of any trouble. I had money, a good home and direction in my life.

Then I changed jobs to be closer to home, and the money I earned meant Jodie and I could afford our drug habit.

Jodie and I stayed together for seven years but we had arguments over drugs, and eventually broke up.

I lost my job and started stealing again. I met up with my friends, the wrong crowd, and got into deep trouble. The police picked me up and questioned me about all sorts of crimes, most of which I knew about, 'cos I did them. They offered me TICs (Taking into Considerations – which is a system by which you get a reduced sentence for helping the police clear up other crimes) if I admitted to the crimes, which I did. I got a four-year sentence.

I served some of my sentence at Guys Marsh prison, where I got into fights over drugs, because I was stupid and unemployed. But one day they shipped me out to Camp Hill prison, where I worked on the machines sewing laundry kit bags, and I spent two years in Camp Hill. When I was released I went back to Wales where I got a job and met up with my real father.

He tried putting me on the right path. He gave me a job and rented me a house.

I got off the drugs just before I met Michelle and passed my provisional oral motorbike test – this meant I could drive a bike under 125cc. I went to work for my father in his security company, and Michelle got pregnant.

Everything was going well until I received a call to say that Michelle had had a miscarriage.

I just lost it.

I went back on drugs, left home and went driving by myself on the bike. The police picked me up for no insurance and banned me from driving for eighteen months. I ignored the ban and still drove the bike. I was high on drugs and beyond caring.

That's when the accident happened.

I was speeding down a road with lots of parked cars. A woman driving in the opposite direction panicked and tried to avoid me. She veered into the parked cars to her left, bounced off them and zig-zagged into more on the right.

I dodged through the gap and was OK, but she had back and neck injuries. I stopped the bike and phoned for an ambulance and the operator phoned the police, who got there first. I was arrested and charged with dangerous driving. It took six months to go to court and I was placed on bail at Michelle's house.

Michelle and I got back together. She said she understood why I'd been so upset. I also managed to get my job back.

Michelle soon got pregnant again.

We were lucky this time. We have a son called Isaac who is now two and a half years old. I had to serve a twelve-month sentence for the accident but I got tagged and was let out.

And I thought everything was OK; I went back to work and started to relax.

Only one night when I was at home playing on my PlayStation the police arrived and shouted, "Open up! We want to talk to you."

I ran away through bushes and across fields. I was scared of what the police would do if they caught me. When I got back to the house they were waiting for me and I was arrested.

I was recalled to prison on burglary charges, but these have now been dropped and I'm waiting to go home to be with Michelle and Isaac.

What I haven't mentioned is that when I was growing up I was unable to read or write.

This changed when I was brought to Parc on 29 April 2008.

I couldn't get a job in the prison because I couldn't read or write. I was stuck in my cell doing nothing, which made me feel bored.

I was sharing my cell with another inmate called Andy; Andy started teaching me how to read. He got me on to education, that's when tutors Jane and Denise started to teach me.

I wanted to stop relying on others to write my letters because I was fed up with other people writing their versions.

I started reading and enjoying the Quick Read books. They have given me the confidence to go home and read aloud to my son Isaac before he goes to bed.

The Love of My Life

Bobby Singh

Arranged marriages are part of my Sikh upbringing.

Usually both sets of parents have known each other for many years. If they haven't, discussions and talks are held to understand the background of the families involved.

My mum and dad had a marriage arranged over the phone. Their parents talked to each other and were happy that they came from good families and had respectable backgrounds. Mum was from London and Dad from Manchester, three hundred and thirty miles apart. When they got married the celebrations lasted for a week. Dad's family travelled to London with one hundred friends and family. They've described it as the happiest day of their life.

For the first few years Mum and Dad lived in Manchester, where I was born, along with my brother and sister. A little later Dad made the decision to move to London where there were better job prospects. In London they had another three children, all boys.

The downside to this was I missed my gran. We were very close, and as a child I would lie beside her all night. She meant the world to me. I was her Bobby Charlton. I will never forget the day she passed away; it felt like my life was over too. My parents told me that my gran would always be with me and to remember the wonderful times we'd had together. It's true I can still smell her around me; she smells of flowers … roses.

I had a brilliant upbringing.

However, I was never into education. All I wanted to do was to go to work and provide for my future family, and from an early age I knew I would be married young. I wanted to make sure my children would never go without, because I never did.

For many years when I was in school I worked in a shop called C&A in Peckham. I would start at 6 a.m. stacking shelves and cleaning till 9.15, which left me 15 minutes to get to school, a ten-minute walk away.

I was good at two lessons – maths and cookery.

During that time I started to mix with the wrong crowd and started to smoke, which was against my religion. It was very hard to keep it from my family, but I did for a long time.

Then I started going out with a white girl, and within weeks we fell in love. But I always knew it couldn't last because we were from different backgrounds; our cultures were different. However, we stayed friends during and after our school years together.

My parents would not have been happy with me if they had found out. I knew that I would have to marry a Sikh girl. It was often hard to accept, but I would never have considered letting my family down.

After I left school I decided to become a chef. I went to college and started to learn how to cook in Café Rouge, which was part of a large chain of restaurants. I was a trainee chef and got on well with everyone.

I passed my driving test and had my own car; life was good, and I fell in love with a Portuguese woman.

We met at work; she had come to England on a six-month visa to provide for her family in Portugal. I asked her out for a drink and was amazed to find that we had the same feelings for each other. We had three wonderful months together, then parted on good terms. She understood the importance of my parents' wish for an arranged marriage.

Two months later I was made redundant.

Because I was seventeen and the eldest son, my parents thought it was time to arrange my marriage. I was always prepared for this but didn't think it would be so soon.

Mum and Dad started looking for a wife for me. I met a few girls; there was nothing wrong with them, except they were not the ones for me. I was looking for a woman with a personality, who could look after my family and our future kids. I thought I was asking for too much until I met Jaskiren.

Jaskiren was from Portsmouth. Our families were good friends, which made a big difference. As soon as I saw her I knew she was the one for me. We had so much in common. She was very good-looking, and still is, with long black hair, dark brown eyes and a perfect smile. I fell in love on the spot and kept saying to myself: you are one lucky guy if she says yes to you.

We stayed in contact by phone. Both of us were excited knowing we would be spending the rest of our lives together.

The date our parents decided on was the 6th December. I couldn't wait, and we both helped our families to arrange things just the way we wanted. The week before the big day my family started to turn up at my home, everyone dressed in bright-coloured clothes.

My parents had hired a marquee and we celebrated by eating homemade food – tandoori chicken, curried goat, lamb meatballs, dahl, okra curry, rice and naan bread. We drank, danced and sang traditional songs. It was great having fun with my cousins as a single man, but all I had on my mind was my wife-to-be, Kiran. I've never seen my parents so happy.

On the night before the wedding a traditional henna party was arranged. One at a time men and women, starting with the oldest member of the family, all rubbed henna into my hands and feet. At the same time everyone sang for hours: religious songs with the words of our gods in them. Some of the men prepared the food for our journey to Portsmouth the following morning, while others danced and played Punjabi music.

I was woken up early on the day of my wedding. The Parti, a priest, performed a religious ceremony, as yogurt and haldi paste were smoothed over my body. I could only take a bath after my sister had washed my hair.

When I had washed and felt fresh my mum's brother presented me with a gold ring, which I wear next to my wedding finger.

To bring me good luck as I started a new life as a family man, everything I wore on my big day was new. I had to give away all my old clothes to my brothers and cousins.

When I was dressed, Dad tied up my turban and Mum gave me gold rings and chains to wear. A traditional decoration made out of flowers covered my face, a religious orange cloth was tied around my waist, and finally a long chain was placed around my neck, which was then stapled with money from my family. This was to ensure I got a good start in my married life.

Everyone then stood and prayed to our god Gurunaka for a good day and a blessed future.

Before we left London I had to sit on a decorated white horse, which was then transported to Portsmouth. This was also part of the traditional Sikh ceremony, to bring me luck. My younger brother was my best man, so it was his responsibility to keep me safe throughout the day. All our neighbours came out into the street to celebrate. The family danced around me, while a man played a big drum called a Duol with two wooden sticks.

Family and friends got on to the hired coaches. They'd even organised a chauffeur-driven limo to bring my loving wife back to London with me.

The party continued when we stopped for a break on our journey. Food prepared from the night before was served. Although I ate, all I was really interested in was seeing Kiran again.

At last we arrived at Kiran's home. My family prayed and danced outside the house and my future brother-in-law escorted me in. His mother had to lift the veil of flowers from my face, and then she kissed my forehead, gave me her blessing and welcomed me into her family. We were all given Indian sweets to celebrate, then were served a full English breakfast.

At last we made our way to the temple, the Gurdwara. It was finally time to marry my bride. I still remember standing there watching Kiran walk towards me dressed in her traditional red clothes. I couldn't believe how lucky I was.

We had our English service first, then said our vows and exchanged wedding rings. I asked my mum, is she all mine now? She laughed and said that was just the beginning – you have to have your Indian blessing now.

During the Indian blessing, we both had to sit down in front of a holy man who read from our religious book. My mum tied the cloth from around my waist to Kiran's. We then had to turn around together seven times and on the seventh turn both sides of the family threw flowers over us. That's when I knew I was married.

I had the biggest smile on my face and thanked God for his blessing.

Just as I thought it was over, we were told we had to sit back down, so our family and friends could bless us with gifts of money. All I wanted to do was kiss my wife.

Our families had hired a hall and caterers for the huge reception party. We danced, ate and drank. Everyone was enjoying themselves. The DJ played my favourite Indian songs and soul music and I was told not to drink too much because I had to go back to Kiran's house for another traditional ceremony. It was already a bit late! I had to slow down!

Traditional games were organised when we arrived back at Kiran's home. One of the games involved her cousins hiding my shoes and me paying for them to be given back. I had no choice but to pay. I was getting a bit fed up by now, but my mum and sister told me to take it easy. I knew I had drunk a bit too much and was tired. They replied that a wife was not easy to get. I now know that.

It was after midnight by the time we were ready to leave for London. Kiran and her family were in floods of tears. It was an emotional time, leaving Portsmouth. We all hugged her, reassuring her that she wasn't alone and that we were her family too.

By now I was exhausted and fell asleep during our journey home.

We arrived in London to find my family and friends were already outside the house, still drinking and singing. Everyone welcomed my new wife as she was carried out of the limo into her new home.

I thought it was all over, but it wasn't. Mum said we had to play some more traditional games. I didn't mind, it was fun. Two hours later I was allowed to go to bed, alone. My mum told me Kiran needed to rest. I asked, what about me? She replied that Kiran would be spending the rest of her life with me.

The following day we had to go back to Portsmouth for more blessings. At last on the way we had the opportunity to talk about our pasts and share our dreams for the future. I didn't want the journey to end. That's when I knew God made Kiran just for me.

When we finally arrived home again we had a nice surprise: my bedroom was filled with presents and the room had been decorated in traditional colours. Also, long strips of flowers had been hung up and petals were scattered on the bed.

Thank God, we were at last left alone. That was our first night together as a couple. Till the day I die it will always be our secret.

When our first baby was born we called her Sukchan after my gran from Manchester. It feels like Gran has come back into my life. I have four children now, Sukchan, Suraj, Simran and Sandeep. When my son Suraj was born I had someone to carry on my name. All of our children mean the world to us.

I have always been a family man. We have our own house and I had good managerial jobs, but in life there are always surprises.

Kiran and I have been married for fifteen

years. Over the years we have been through a lot and have always stood by one another.

My biggest mistake was to get into trouble with the police, and be put in this place, but I know the love of my life, Kiran, will always be out there waiting for me.

A Troubled Man

Shuhel

I'll start this short story about my life by introducing myself. My name is Shuhel. I was born in 1982 in the heart of England. London was the city of my birth and I'm really proud of that even though my parents are Asians and from Bangladesh.

I am the second of three children. We were a very close family. I have an older brother and a younger sister but I was the most loved. I had everything I wanted and was very close to my dad. I remember playing wrestling, football and many other games with him. To me he was the best dad in the world. Not to forget my mother; she was everything you would want a mother to be: loving, caring, over-protective.

At age ten my life took a turn for the worse. My family did not have a great deal of money, but my father always got everything that everyone wanted. I remember one night, late, I was watching TV in the sitting room and I heard the front door open. It was my dad coming back from work. He came into the room, sat me on his lap and called my mum. He told her he had been made bankrupt. I didn't know what bankrupt meant, but looking back I know my dad had lost his restaurant. And he couldn't go to work any more because he had high blood pressure.

I told him not to worry. I said I would pray to God for him to get better.

Then one day we were all in town and I saw some trainers I really liked. I asked my father to buy them for me but he said he didn't have enough money. I went home feeling really angry. I had become very selfish. On another occasion – it was Eid, the Muslim festival after the end of Ramadan – my father only gave me £5 to spend, when he used to give me £10. All my friends would have at least £10. I went into my mum's pocket, stole another £5, and went out for the day. Coming back I felt guilty and was getting ready to say sorry, but as no one said anything I guessed that my mum and dad had thought they had spent it.

I started stealing regularly. I got caught and apologised but did it again and again. At High

School my attitude became really bad; I was disrespectful to the teachers and started truanting from lessons. I took my first puff of a cigarette; I thought that in order to get respect I would have to do this. That was the biggest mistake of my entire life and if there was one thing I could change it would be that. Truanting and smoking had now got me hanging with the wrong crowd and soon enough I started using cannabis. Smoking cannabis was fun at the time – it made me feel immortal. It felt like total freedom from the world. But because of this I ended up getting expelled from High School. And to be honest I didn't really care because I knew my life was heading for danger. I was a street boy now, hanging, or should I say chilling, doing nothing but smoking cannabis on street corners. I even started hating the police.

Soon after the age of twenty, my life hit another low; I was introduced to Class A drugs by one of my close mates. I had no income and plenty of people in the area were addicted to Class A drugs such as crack and heroin. I knew that selling drugs was not right because I was raised by a good family who taught me right from wrong, but something at the back of my head was saying that this was my road to riches and nothing could stop me. I got some heroin off a mate and started selling it to people on the streets of Cardiff. I also took a puff of it now and then. My family started noticing things about my behaviour. I was more arrogant, I owned things I couldn't afford, such as the car my father saw me driving. I didn't have a licence, either.

My father asked me about all this and I couldn't answer him. The last words he said to me were that one day I would receive punishment for selling and taking drugs. I thought that maybe he was right but I was so deep in I couldn't get out. I owed, and was owed, money. I realised that this drugs business was asking for something bad to happen to me.

So I decided to get away and go to Bangladesh for some time, to find a good wife and come back and start all over again with a clean sheet.

I stepped out of the plane and there I was, far from my problems in a distant land, my motherland, the lovely blue country of Bangladesh. The skies were blue and the scenery was breathtaking. On my arrival no one recognised me because I'd changed my image from an eastern to a western look. My uncle, who was at the airport to pick me up, was very pleased to see me. We went back to my village and had a big feast.

The next morning, in front of me was an army of cousins and relatives I never knew existed, one saying, 'I am your auntie', five saying they were my uncles and about twenty-odd claiming to be my cousins, sisters and brothers!

I knew it was time for me to settle down, so one day I set off to town to buy some CDs – in other words, to look for girls. As I was walking around, I could see some stunning girls but they were hard to approach because the girls here had more self-respect and didn't allow themselves to be chatted up. I told a close relative of mine about my situation, that I needed to find a wife because I needed some responsibilities in life, and that I'd made my final decision to get married. We went to many villages asking if there were any good brides, obviously virgins with a natural beauty, and who were, most importantly, respectful to their parents. Luck was on my side – I found a pretty girl who met all the criteria I was looking for. We got together on several occasions, discovered we were right for each other and decided to get married.

So that's what I did. I got married to a lovely girl who respected and loved me and I came back to the UK. At that time I was twenty-two. I kept a low profile and my dad bought me a take-away restaurant. I was working like any other person and at the end of the week I would give the profit from the business to my family. I felt really good that I was now taking care of my family and providing for them. I thought I had my life back again.

But waiting round the corner was my worst nightmare. One day I was getting stock for my take-away and I bumped into somebody I owed money to. He was not happy. I told him that I had changed my ways and started a new life but to him it meant nothing. He said he wanted his money and he wanted it in a month. For a minute I was lost; I couldn't pay him. I owed him £3000 and there was no way I was going to take money out of the business. I decided to phone him and propose that I take drugs to sell and pay him back in full until the debt cleared. Surprisingly, he agreed. So I was selling drugs again, and yes, I was using as well. It took me three months to pay him back. The debt was over and I was relieved. But there was one problem: I had become a drug addict.

I ended up not taking care of business properly and eventually my dad decided to sell the take-away. My life became a mess and I was lost. I used more drugs to get me out of my misery and, after all my money was finished, my wife told me she was pregnant. I felt numb – I had a drug habit and no money. Now what would I do? I really believed that my life was over and I was taking two other people down with me, my wife and unborn child. I kept asking, is this my destiny, a life of misery? Two steps forward and three steps back, I was achieving nothing in the long run.

I ended up working for someone else in a restaurant. I was the head chef there, but I still had a habit and a family to feed; the money I was earning was not enough for both. On one of my days off work I sat down for hours, thinking about how to make ends meet. How was I going to give up drugs? How was I going to move up in life? What were my options? After long deep thought I came to the ultimate master plan: I would carry on working in the night but sell drugs during the day. That way I could make money, I wouldn't have to pay for my drug habit and within two years I could get my own business. I would also have money for treatment. This was now make or break for me.

I got some drugs and started selling again. It was going well. I paid the dealer back and I was buying the drugs with cash now. It was looking good. I used to wake up, sell drugs till 4 p.m., hand the phone and the drugs over to a friend and go to work. While I was working, my friend was making money for me. At the end of the night I would collect the drugs, the money and the phone. This carried on for about five months and I saved up a bit of money.

One day, my phone rang early in the morning. It was a customer for heroin, so I went out. When I came back I knew that something wasn't right, but I didn't let it bother me. Three days later the police bust down my front door and found money, drugs and two phones. There was nothing I could do. I was remanded and convicted of supplying Class A drugs and was sentenced to four years in prison.

In prison I received the news that my wife had given birth to a girl.

I am twenty-six now. Another year and a half

behind bars and I'm a free man. I've got my wife behind me and a lovely daughter to look after. I can't afford to lose them now. I do regret everything that has happened to me but I can only blame myself. I've been drug-free for some time now. I know I can't change the past but what can change is the future. Coming to prison has changed my life; I can now honestly say I've learnt my lesson and that when I get out all that will be on my mind is my little girl. I have to live like a normal person and look after my family. I went through hell and back and I'm not risking it again and putting my girl's future on the line. One thing I will always remember: "Good things come to those who wait".

A Soldier in Prison

Aron

In the summer of 2005 I was serving in Iraq with the 1st Battalion Welsh Guards.

I didn't think anything different about the day. It was seven in the morning, and 3 Platoon's turn on mobile patrol in the Basra outskirts. It was a warm morning with the sun blazing in our eyes. We loaded our weapons and jumped on the Landrovers. We left the camp smoothly without any problems.

Everything felt normal on the patrol. I thought it would be a quiet day – just the noise of cars passing by and people shouting as usual. But suddenly the sound levels seemed to drop and everyone was out of sight – there was just the sound of the 2.0 litre Landrovers revving their engines...I had a gut feeling. I knew something wasn't right.

Then there was an explosion. The noise was indescribable. There was ringing in my ears. I turned around to see that Delta 1, the first Landrover, had been hit. Time stood still. It was as if it wasn't real. A roadside bomb.

We rushed to the vehicle. There was screaming. My section commander, Sergeant Williams, went to the front of the Landrover. The driver, Atwell, couldn't move, he was hurt badly. Miles was fine – he was just in shock. But then I opened the back door and found my good friend Dean lying there, screaming in agony. I knew this was a bad one. The top of his leg had melted to the Landrover's plastic seat. The smell was strong – his flesh was burning up. We told him, "We're going to rip you away!" The Landrover was on fire, so we knew we had to be quick. We ripped him away. He yelped in pain. The noise of ripping skin and flesh lasted about three seconds.

We lifted him out and got away safely. The Landrover blew into a big ball of fire.

We had gone from being a quiet patrol with no problems to the victims of a planned attack within one minute.

That's how fast things can change in Iraq.

It was a dull, dark morning. I didn't want to wake up. I was due in court at ten o'clock. I suddenly thought, how did I get into this mess, going from having a good job and a relatively good life, to losing it all in an instant? I couldn't think straight and the atmosphere between me and my girlfriend Diane was very different to usual. I didn't want any fuss, but Diane's mother, Louise, decided to come along to support me and her daughter. I remember trying to put my tie on, I just couldn't do it. I was severely stressed. I couldn't even eat any breakfast. My stomach felt like it had a rat inside, slowly eating it away. I recall Gruff, Diane's brother, wishing me good luck. It didn't help that it was the day before my nineteenth birthday.

We stepped into the car. The traffic was busy, busier than normal. It felt like hours driving into Swansea, but in reality it was a mere twenty minutes. We decided to stop for breakfast at McDonald's. Louise urged me to eat something, but I still wasn't feeling any easier. My head started to feel light and was overloading with worry.

We arrived at the Crown Court and while I was walking from the car for a split second a thought came into my head: that this might be the last time I walk in Swansea for a while. But I was trying to think positively. I didn't want to face reality. I locked my demons in a cupboard at the back of my head.

I waited anxiously to speak to my barrister. My captain from the army was also attending court to represent me. My barrister couldn't tell me a lot that I didn't already know. We entered the court room, and I felt cold. I wished it was a dream. The barristers and judge were giving information to each other. I wasn't listening; the thoughts in my head were overriding everything.

Finally the judge made his decision. "Nine months." That's all I heard, that's all I wanted to hear. It felt as if someone had ripped my heart out, because I couldn't feel it beating.

I turned around to the public gallery and saw Diane crying her heart out. I was speechless. I spent so much time thinking about myself I hadn't realised how it was hurting other people.

I wasn't very keen on that small confined space in the Reliance van. I'd calmed down, though. What would prison be like?

I walked from the van into the prison reception. I was having hot and cold sweats. But everything was surprisingly normal; the officers spoke to me and treated me fine. I was allowed a quick phone call. I rang Diane's house, and her brother answered and asked if I was OK. "I'm fine," I said. Diane rushed to the phone. I said I loved her and that I was sorry. The call didn't last long. I was feeling rough.

An officer finally walked me to the induction wing where all new prisoners go. I couldn't imagine what it was going to be like. The sky had turned dark and there was a chill in the air. The wing was a lot bigger than I imagined. There was nobody to be seen. I was put on the third floor in cell 73. The door slammed behind me and I was suddenly all alone in this small room with a metal bed and a TV for my entertainment. I was in shock. I couldn't think straight.

Time went on and things got slightly better. I moved to the best wing where it was a lot cleaner. I had a job instantly and was soon mixing in with other inmates. Prison life was surprisingly easy for me. The support of Diane, her family and my family made it a lot easier, too. I'd been sent to jail and there was nothing I could do about it, so I had to get on with it.

Most days were routine. We had two hours association every night and exercise and gym most days. Officers had a very good attitude towards inmates and were happy to help with any issues. I looked forward to my visits and to playing football on the weekends. It's ironic how I used to take small things for granted outside; now I couldn't even walk twenty metres without being escorted. I've tried to do as many courses as I could to benefit me for when I leave.

It's not all been bad. I've learnt a lot about myself and the mistakes I've made and regained my self-respect and respect for others. Now I am approaching the end of my sentence and am feeling a lot better about myself.

Memories

I can't imagine what life is like out there.
Being in here so long, I just can't remember what it was like,

Walking in the park,
Going shopping,
Getting into a car,
Going to a restaurant, going to the pub,
Playing rugby,
Seeing my family,
Meeting my mates,
Going to the cinema,

Tasting that first drop of lager in your mouth,
Taking my dog for a walk,
Hugging my girlfriend,
Sleeping with my girlfriend,
Getting a take-away,
Earning money.
Watching the football LIVE!
Having a hangover from the night before.

Distant memories.

But future realities!

Inside Times

Arif

The first day inside Cardiff prison I was moved on to the detox wing because I was still suffering from the effects of cocaine and alcohol misuse. My cell had a camera fitted in the corner of the wall to check on people who try to commit suicide. Obviously they didn't know that I had been in there before and that I would never harm myself. The first week was hell on that wing. I couldn't sleep for the first four days and even after that I had to take sleeping pills to knock me out. The only good thing about being there was that I was eating well.

The second week was pretty much the same, I twisted and turned in the night, waking up at three or four in the morning thinking I was at home. Then came the day I was moved on to F wing, the main remand wing of Cardiff prison. I was hoping to see someone I knew; you always know someone from the road. Two weeks in I got two'd up with my good friend

Milad, who I'd got to know when I was in Portland doing four years and he was also doing a four for armed robbery. Anyway, I was glad to get two'd up with someone I knew and trusted.

We got on well and we started praying five times a day together, which was good for both of us because on the outside neither of us would pray. His missus would turn up outside the prison every night with the kids to talk to him. She would park up on the pavement opposite the magistrates' court, facing our cell window. He would flick the light on and off three times. When she parked up he would know because she would toot her horn twice. They would shout to each other and tell each other about their day. He would ask her about how she was running his take-away and ask if there were any problems, and his son would shout as loud as he could, "Abba, I love you!" He was only three at the time.

I didn't know what was going happen about my case, and I was stressed out about my beautiful daughter whose birthday was coming up. I wasn't going to be there for a second time. She was going to be three.

Almost every night I would look out from behind the bars of my window up at the stars and imagine times I was with my daughter, playing in the garden with her, when she was in the bath, and the times I used to take her to the park to play on the swings and slides. We used to have so much fun. And then my dream would stop and I would be back in my cell like I had been there for a hundred years.

It's a beautiful day, the 4th of April 2006. Blue skies, no clouds in sight, the sun's out: perfect weather to take my daughter to the park or beach. She would love that. I miss spending time with her so much I would do anything to be with her right now. When I get out I have so much catching up to do. There is so much we have missed out on.

I hope she still recognises me and wants to know me when we meet up, because if she hates me I won't get over it. Every night I dream of going to see Alisha when I get out. It's weird, I'm always outside her nana's house in Purley, Reading, in a car, thinking of going in. Sometimes I go in but don't see her. Her family are there and we don't get on.

Then there's times when I'm angry with them for not letting me stay in contact with her while I'm in prison, as I need to see her or hear her voice.

58

I have realised that this is my last chance to put things right with my family and my daughter. If I don't learn from my mistakes I won't get another chance. I now understand that when I make a mistake or wrong decision it doesn't just affect me but all the people who care about me, most of all my daughter. I have learnt the hard way but I think it's a good thing because now I appreciate life and freedom and I won't do anything to jeopardise it.

The reason I want to write about my life is so that my daughter and her mum can understand why I made the decisions I did, and for them to know how I grew up and the struggle I went through. I want my daughter to know more about me so she can get to understand me, and most of all forgive me.

I grew up without a father. To this day I don't know who he is, where he is, or what he looks like and I still have so many unanswered questions about that side of my family. So I want Alisha to know everything about me: where I've been, where I am and what I want in life, and how much I need her in my life because I don't want to make the same mistake as my father made, abandoning me and not leaving me anything to explain why.

My daughter means everything to me and I can't understand why her mum is not letting me speak to her over the phone or letting me get in contact with her. She knows I am in prison and I am here for a long time, so what harm could it do, me staying in contact with her? I think it would be better if I stayed in contact with her because then she will know where I am and can speak to me regularly and receive letters and pictures on special occasions. At least we would have a link between us and when we meet up it wouldn't be so bad. But at the moment there's nothing between us and when we do meet up in the future she still might not want to know me, or even recognise me.

I know there are a lot of people in worse situations than me in here so I can't really complain. There are people doing life and some people whose families have moved away. They don't even know where they are. Compared to them, I'm all right and I ain't complaining. But I wish things were different.

When I was fourteen I spent a year with a family in Reading, where there were good and bad influences. A guy called Shak was always staying away from school, and we hung around together. It was a posh school, with a uniform, and lots of good facilities. I wasn't used to anything like that; back home in Cardiff I'd gone to Cathays High School, where they had nothing.

At fifteen I was back in Cardiff, but I felt like I didn't fit in there any more. I felt alienated. I had an old friend who was OK, but I also had a lot of enemies. Also, my stepfather was beating me, and I didn't want to go to school with marks on my face. My older brothers couldn't do anything about it. I was good at cheating and pretending that I knew things that I didn't really understand. We'd get into the cupboard and find out the answers to tests. They thought I knew about Shakespeare and maths, x + y and stuff like that. I was in class groups that were too high for me. I didn't admit anything because I didn't want to show myself up, especially in front of the girls!

I had this friend called Fazal. His family owned restaurants up the valleys so he always had plenty of money. His dad would sometimes give him £100 at the weekend. And there was another guy called Karim. We all decided we were going to run away together. We packed some back-packs and set off up the river at Blackwood. But after a little while Fazal wanted to give up and go home. So we did. Of course, I got beaten up for it.

Later, we tried again. This time we were three or four days away. We stayed at my mate's house in Gabalfa. They were sunny days, playing football and hanging around. We'd go down to the school and hang around there. They were making announcements about us at the school. Then one evening we were hanging around a pub in Gabalfa and we saw this white Nissan Micra. I knew it belonged to a friend of my older brother. They saw us and got out and got hold of us. Fazal's mum was there, screaming at us. When I got home I was beaten up again.

Now around this time there were riots going on in the streets and in the schools, between the Asians, Somalis and Whites. Fazal had lots of hobbies – his house was full of games and internet stuff – but one of his hobbies was guns. He knew this guy who ran a store in town, an ex-SAS guy. His speciality was making imitation firearms into useable ones.

A fight had been arranged one night at the back of Lo-Cost on Crwys Road; a fight against the docks boys, the Somali boys. They were known as the Warriors, or the Smiling Boys. Fazal was really steaming, really angry. Somebody had thrown a brick through his mum's window or something. We went down there with two guns that Fazal had got from the guy at the store. There were forty to fifty Somali boys there with baseball bats, and lots of girls were there to watch what happened. There were four or five of us. There were also two younger boys, about thirteen to fourteen years old, who had a knife, but they ran off pretty soon. Suddenly, Fazal fired the guns and hit a few cars. We all ran off, and dumped the guns in an alleyway. But then we decided to go back to get them.

There were some white guys sitting in the car park, mouthing off. One was a tougher-looking guy, a skinhead. The rest walked off. The skinhead was wearing a big black coat. He was walking towards us and I could tell he had something under his coat. There were only three of us now. He pulled out a golf club, one of those with a big head on the end of it: a driver. He started swinging it. We ran down a dead-end street which had a garage at the end. The mosque was there. Fazal pulled a piece of pipe out of a skip. Me and Fazal went for him, but he hit me, and seriously hurt my shoulder.

I rolled underneath a car. He was trying to kick me. I had a knife and pulled it out. Then he went for my friend Mossad. Mossad's face was covered in blood. I was suddenly out from under the car and I came up behind him and stabbed him, in the lower back.

He screamed – I'll never forget it – and fell to the floor with the knife stuck in him. Fazal was yelling at me, "Pull the knife out! Pull the knife out!" I pulled it out, and as we were near the mosque I threw it on the roof. The younger guys were back now and were kicking him; they didn't know that he'd been stabbed. Me and Fazal were yelling, "Leave him!" We ran, and jumped over a railway fence and ended up in Mackintosh Place. We were freaking out, as what we had done sank in. We ran towards the flower gardens, by St David's College.

When I got home it was strange. My family were pleased to see me. They were happy I was home! They gave me and my brother money to go and play pool. The next day we set off down the road to City Snooker. Outside were two guys sitting in a car, and when we came out the two guys started following us. My brother was getting suspicious. "Arif," he said to me, "what have you done?" I didn't tell him, and the two guys got into a car and drove away. But when we got to the house, a car was there. A riot van.

That night everyone was arrested, in armed raids. Doors were forced open all over Cardiff. At the police stations, parents were beating their children in front of the police. Fazal grassed me up. He didn't say anything about the guy from the store, of course, because he knew the man would kill him. Said he'd got the guns off the internet. The skinhead was in intensive care.

It was a big case, lots of witnesses. I was done for GBH (grievous bodily harm), affray and abuse of a firearm. But for some reason the police said that blanks were fired, which they weren't. Perhaps they didn't want to spread the word that people were using guns and inflame the trouble. My brother was the only person there for me in court. The court was full of people and the girls from the car park were shouting abuse. I got four years but the rest were also sent down. The judge reckoned they were guilty, too.

My Life in Prison

Marcus

When I left court for prison there were so many things going through my head: how was I going to manage? Would I get beaten up? Was I going to be a victim of racism?

When I got there it was about 7.30 p.m. on a Monday night. I was put in a cell with a guy from Bristol; we talked all night about a lot of things, and he told me what he had done and I told him my story as well. He told me that tomorrow he would be going into a single cell. He felt that if he stayed with me he would stress me out because he had a lot on his mind: his girl was pregnant and he couldn't take it. Anyway, the next morning I was up early. I couldn't sleep; there was so much on my mind from the night before.

After breakfast I had a shower. A guy came up to me asking for burn (another name for tobacco in prison) but I told him no, I didn't smoke. He asked me what I was in for and I told him. We started talking. He said: let's go to a table. He told me a lot about prison, that I must not be afraid if the other prisoners took the piss or bullied me. Our conversation lasted for the rest of the association.

I was in my cell one afternoon when an officer opened the door and asked if I would like to go into a double cell. I didn't hesitate because I was really stressing on my own. So he told me to pack my stuff and go downstairs to cell 30.

I finished packing and went to cell number 30 as I was told. The door was open. There was an inmate inside with a mop and a bucket, cleaning it out. As I was about to say something, the same officer approached and shouted to the other inmate, "Owen, this is your new cellmate." Owen looked at me and gave me his hand to shake, as they always do.

After I'd walked in, the officer shut the cell door and said, "Good luck, lads." I put my stuff on the bed and started to unpack. While I was making my bed, Owen finally said something to me.

"Where are you from?"

"London."

"How come you are in here?"

"I got caught in Cardiff."

He told me he was from Cardiff, that he was nineteen years old and on remand for supplying Class A drugs. He was short, medium-built and of mixed race; he told me his dad was black and his mother white.

I carried on making my bed while he was cleaning the toilet area. As he came out to wash his hands, he took off his jumper. I was shocked to see his arms – they had lots of cuts and bruises. I wanted to ask him what had happened to his arms, but I didn't know how he would take it.

While he was washing his hands, I could see how horrible the slices looked, like he had been in a sword-fight with someone. I couldn't hold my thoughts any longer, so I asked him what had happened.

He looked at me, then took up his towel and wiped his hands. He didn't say a word for about two minutes. As he took the towel from his face, I was wondering what his reaction was going to be. Then he asked, "You really want to know?"

"If it's not a problem to you," I replied.

"I sliced myself up."

"With what?"

He paused, then smiled a bit and said, "A blade."

"Why?" I asked.

He started to tell me how stressed he was after he got locked up and his mother didn't want to accept his phone calls. He said he'd done it about three days ago. I knew he didn't want to talk more about it so I just sat on my bed and started to watch TV. We never exchanged another word about it.

We were both unlocked for association that evening and, as usual, I took out my towel and gel to have a shower. Owen went over to the phone. For the whole of association I didn't see Owen until the officers called ten minutes to bang-up, when I saw him running towards our cell. He came out with his cup.

"Do you want a cup of hot water?" he asked.

"I'm fine."

"Don't you drink at night?"

"I don't mind."

Owen came in and shut the door behind him. I was watching TV. He made his tea and said nothing.

The hours went by and my eyes felt sleepy. I asked Owen if he was watching TV.

"Switch it off."

I said my regular prayer before I closed my eyes. But for the whole night I couldn't get to sleep; every twenty minutes the light would come on and I could hear someone at the door. There were times when I would look over at him on his bed and he would be well asleep; it looked like I was the only one affected by this. I couldn't sleep. I was frustrated. I just lay there looking at the roof, saying to myself, "This is not my night".

The next morning, when we got up for breakfast, I told him that I hadn't slept, that the light kept going on and off, and that there was always someone looking through the hole at us. "That's bad," he said, "because it was the best rest I've had since I've been locked up!" I smiled and walked away to the servery for my breakfast.

I bumped into an officer called Jones. Mr Jones was well known to me; he was always polite.

"Good morning, sir."

"Good morning!"

"Last night my cell lights were going on and off every twenty minutes. Why is that?"

"Are you in a double cell?"

"Yes."

He told me to go and get my breakfast, then

he would explain everything to me. I sat at the table to eat my toast and cereal.

"Sorry."

"What for?"

"We have to keep watch on your cellmate."

"But why?"

"He's a self-harmer."

I swallowed my saliva and took a deep breath. I looked at Mr Jones and wondered how I was going to get out of that cell.

"Can I be removed?"

"No. Not at the moment."

"But I couldn't sleep last night."

"I'll see what I can do for you."

Breakfast time was up and I ran back to my cell. I saw Owen looking through the window. He was crying.

"What's the matter, Owen?"

"I can't take this!" he shouted.

"Calm down," I whispered.

"I can't calm down. This place is doing my head."

He turned to face me and I saw he had a piece of blade in his hand. That was when I started to fear for my life, because he had a weird look in his eye. The cell door was closed and I couldn't run.

I acted brave. "Put down the blade, Owen.

Let's talk."

"I don't want to talk," he muttered.

"At this moment, Owen, you are stressing me out and I've got problems of my own."

With relief I heard keys shaking along the landing. An officer was coming. Owen hid the blade. The door opened.

"Mr Owen Price!" shouted the officer.

"Yes?"

"Come with me."

"Where?" Owen was wiping his tears away.

"There's a psychiatrist here to see you."

He walked off, and the officer looked at me and asked if I was alright. I told him yes, but I guessed that he must have seen my shocked expression. He closed the cell door and left.

Sitting on my own in the cell, many thoughts went through my head. Finally I jumped off my bed and went for the blade. I'd seen where he'd hidden it – in the bed-box.

I threw the blade through the window, then rang the intercom and asked to speak with Mr Jones. He wasn't in. Another officer, Mr Jackson, came.

"What's wrong, boy?"

"I need to get out of this cell."

"Do you have a problem?"

"Yes I do."

I was told to pack my stuff, which I did quickly. Mr Jackson took me to another cell. I was overjoyed; I was out of that mad cell at last. But as I sat in my new cell alone, I couldn't help thinking about what had happened to Owen, because I knew he needed help.

As the months went by, I would often see Owen when I went to play football. He would always be at the fence looking at the game. I haven't spoken to him since I left that cell, because he was moved to another wing. I heard that he had a four-year sentence, which makes me wonder if he is still a self-harmer and how he is coping now.

I have been in for four months now and I have seen a lot of things. One day this guy on the third floor climbed up on the pipes and threatened to jump if the officers didn't meet his request, which was to change cells. It was frightening. I just looked up to the sky and said a prayer.

And I've been in one fight, which will definitely be my last. I was working in the industries department, packing teabags for the wings in the prison. The shop that I work in has about twenty inmates, but I was the only one from London. Most were from Bristol, Cardiff, Swansea and Newport.

Anyway, we started working about nine o'clock in the morning. I work with two guys on the table packing sugars. I took a break and went to the toilets for a while. After I finished I washed my hands and got back to my work area. About two minutes later, this guy came up to the table I was working on. He was a massive-looking guy about twenty-five years old and looked like a rugby player. He was from an adult wing. He asked me if I had just used the toilet.

"Yes," I answered.

"Man, your shit stinks."

"It's meant to, and is it a problem for you?"

"Don't get cheeky!" he yelled.

He walked back to the table that he was working on and started to talk with the three guys he was with. They all started laughing as if he was telling them jokes. Then he suddenly shouted out so everyone in the workshop could hear. "Your shit smells like spoiled eggs."

It wasn't funny to me so I said, "Shut up and act your age."

"Who are you talking to like that?" he asked.

"You!" I shouted.

He grabbed a handful of sugars from my table.

"You little rat."

"Why don't you go back to your table and do some work?"

"Don't talk down to me, you stinking bastard."

"You are a stupid and childish guy for your age."

He paused for a while without saying a word. Then suddenly everyone started to laugh at him. I could see changes in his face. He just stood staring at me. Then he threw his packets in my face.

The workshop went quiet. I sat still with a smile on my face wondering what to do. Then I got up from the table, staring at him, and laughing as if it was funny.

"Let's see how you like that," he said.

I stepped closer to him. I could feel the tension rising between us.

"What are you going to do about that?" he asked.

I punched him on the left side of his face. I was shocked; I never knew I could hit someone so hard. He almost fell to the ground, holding his face.

"Come on! Come on, you bastard!" he

raged. Then he was running around like a boxer.

If only he'd known that mine was a coward punch. I just stood there watching, anticipating what he was going to do.

"Lucky punch!" he yelled.

I knew I couldn't fight him, but still I didn't move.

"One punch knock-out. Come on!"

He must have repeated that ten times, while running around like Frank Bruno. Luckily the instructor returned and pulled him away. I felt like a free bird. Three other officers came in and one took me to a room, while he was led off in a different direction.

When I returned to the workshop, all the guys started shouting, "Good punch! Good punch!" The instructor called me over and asked me what I would have done if he had punched me back. Bravely I replied, "Fight him!" He said that often big guys tried to bully the smaller ones, when in fact they couldn't fight.

It was a shock to me that the big guy never did a thing after I hit him. Now I realise that size doesn't matter. It was the first time I had ever punched someone.

How I Ended Up the Way I Am

Patrick

My name is Patrick. I am twenty-five years old and I am writing this so that people will understand why I have ended up in prison, how I lost my freedom and also, most importantly, how I lost my family and the respect of the people who mean the most to me.

At the age of six I was taken away from my family and placed into local authority care; this was because my father was an alcoholic and he had a bad temper. Me and my brother Darren were placed with a foster carer in Bath. This was a long way away from our family but at least we were together. We were able to see our mother and father once every six weeks to start with, which was nice, but when the time came for them to go we found it very hard and upsetting, and it took a long time for us to get used to it.

The foster carer found me a school close to where we lived but my brother Darren had to go to a different school, which was around ten miles away. I found it hard being away from the only person that truly loved and cared for me. After a number of weeks my brother was moved back to Bristol and I was all alone; it was a very hard time. Over the next couple of months I was assaulted physically and mentally by my carers, which lead to my behaviour deteriorating and me skipping school and getting into trouble. I started to hang around with the wrong type of people.

By the age of fourteen I had started to use drugs and to get into trouble. I was moved back to Bristol and placed in a children's home where my behaviour continued to get worse and I lost all respect for people and property. When I turned seventeen I met the mother of my daughter Jo, and we were together for around two and a half years, till I ended up in prison with a four-year sentence.

I thought a lot while I was in prison about my family and my daughter and how much I had missed out on. When I was released just three days before my twenty-first birthday, I had to stay in a hostel for a number of weeks to be assessed by probation officers to make sure that I was complying with my licence. I was trying to put my life back together which was harder than I thought, but I had loving relatives to help and support me which gave me a safety net in case things went wrong.

After my attempts to rebuild my relationship with my daughter's mother fell through, I tried to continue my life as best I could. I found a job as a chef which gave me high hopes for the future, but there was bad news on the way: my father was taken into hospital with heart problems and, after a number of weeks, he passed away.

The death of my father hit me hard. It felt like there was no hope for me and that I was never going to be able to move on with my life. For many weeks I was in a deep dark place. Help came in the form of my brother Darren. Even though he was grieving too, he somehow found the strength to help me overcome my depression. If it were not for my brother's help I might not be here today and might not have been able to write this story.

My life started to look up. I decided to go back to chef work at a local restaurant on the waterfront in Bristol. I was trying my best to improve myself so that when I had the chance to see Jo she would be proud of her father, proud that I was able to settle down and find a decent job and a nice house,

I finally had a chance to see my daughter for the first time in over four years and I wanted to make a good impression. I worried that she did not know who I was. When I arrived at my ex-partner's house I got out of my car and walked slowly towards her front door. My heart was racing and my palms were sweaty.

I took a deep breath and knocked on the door. My ex-partner answered the door and invited me in. I saw the most beautiful girl in the world looking at me. I dropped to one knee and she ran over to me and gave me a big cuddle. At that moment I was the happiest father in the world.

But two weeks later I received a phone call from my ex-partner informing me that she didn't want me to see my daughter again. I asked her why but she didn't say. I told her that it wasn't fair on Jo, especially now, after such a long time of not seeing each other. I told her that it would break Jo's heart and that there was a chance that Jo would blame herself and might think that she had done something wrong. But this didn't seem to matter to her. So I decided that, just to keep the peace, I would respect her wishes.

December 24th came in next to no time. I decided to work late because I couldn't face being alone. I stayed at work till around 1 a.m. then I decided to go to a nightclub for a few drinks. Before I knew it, it was close to 6 a.m. so I headed home to bed. I woke up around 8 p.m. on Christmas night. I felt low and depressed because I hadn't heard from my daughter and I also couldn't get though to her on the phone. I went back to sleep.

I awoke the next morning feeling a lot better now that Christmas was over. I was due back in work later that day. After work I headed home with only one thing on my mind: my daughter Jo and my feelings of hatred for her mother for stopping her seeing me. I couldn't understand why she had done this to us. Couldn't she see that this was affecting Jo's behaviour both at home and at school? Couldn't she see that there was a chance that Jo might blame herself for her mother's decision?

The New Year was upon us and I made a promise to myself that I would try my best to have contact with my daughter, so that she would have the chance to get to know me better. I contacted a solicitor, and he told me that I would have to go through the local family courts.

But after the court case was over I had a bad feeling. I received a letter from my solicitor stating that the court had denied my application due to the fact that I had been in prison for a gun crime and the judge thought that I was a threat to the public. So he'd turned down my application for a visiting order.

I went home and cried myself to sleep and woke the next morning feeling low and depressed. But I knew that I had to get out of this state of mind. I decided to go to work; it was my day off but I had to do something to clear my mind. The boss said that I could do an extra shift and for this I was thankful.

The weeks passed quickly and soon it was summer My mother was taken ill and rushed to hospital with a chest infection. Me, my new girlfriend and my brother Darren dashed to the hospital to see her. When we arrived the nurse told us that there wasn't anything to worry about and that Mum would be fine, they just wanted to keep her in for a couple of days for observation. So we gave our mother a kiss and left her to rest.

A few days later we received a phone call from the hospital informing us that our mother had caught the MRSA. bug! We headed to the hospital straight away. When we arrived the nurse told us that she had shown signs of improvement. This was a great relief to us all, so later in the day we left her so that she could rest.

Later that night, at about 10.15 p.m., I felt a cold shiver down my back. Not long after, my brother Darren received a phone call from the hospital. His face went white and his eyes started to water. I asked him what was wrong. He looked back at me and I asked him if Mum had died. He threw down his phone, jumped up and hugged me. We both cried for a very long time, then headed to the hospital. I can't explain why, but we felt that we had to be where our mum was.

After we buried our mother I went through a bad depression and I started to use heroin. Instead of dealing with the loss of the most important lady in my life, the drugs took over my life and destroyed me from the inside out. This was a major factor in why my girlfriend and I argued so much – without realising it, I was treating her really badly.

When I didn't have the money for drugs I would argue with my girlfriend and then go out and rob people. On one occasion I stole a handbag from a house which belonged to an old lady – this is the reason I am in prison this time, doing a two-year sentence, and this is the reason I wasn't able to be at the birth of my son who was born on the 3rd of March. It is now the 4th of June. I still haven't been able to see him and this has really hurt me, as it would anyone.

I am now sitting in prison with just a few photos of my son. All that is keeping me going is the thought that I will be able to see and hold him soon. My experience is one that I wouldn't wish any of my children to go though, and that is why I am writing this – so that my children can see why I have ended up in prison.

I would just like to add that I have lost so much while I have been in here: respect, love, honour, trust, dignity and a lot more. I have let down the people that I love and who love me and I am on the verge of losing the chance of bringing up my son. I just hope that I am given the chance to prove that I can be a good dad, and that I am able to provide a warm, loving and safe environment for my son.

2006 Temporary Release

Tom

I waited in the cold wind and drizzly rain, wearing only a T-shirt. The main gate warden approached me with his overlapped belly and his bright yellow raincoat.

"Name?"

"Tom, boss."

"Number?"

"FD4573."

"Where are you going?"

"CSV Bettws, boss." (That's Community Service Volunteers, to you.)

My stomach started to tremble. The boss returned to his cabin. The tall steel gates began to open sideways.

I began to move slowly towards the outside world. I felt myself shaking.

The gates closed. I was left there standing, viewing the green, misty hills.

Thoughts ran through my mind:

You can go home ...
You can go anywhere ...
You're in freedom ...

My lift pulled up to the side of me. My CSV officer sat there with her long, brunette hair and smelling of some strong, beautiful fragrance.

I felt a little nervous. Had that cold feeling again.

I opened the car door ...

"Hi."

"Hiya," Marianne said. "Sorry I'm late."

I sat down on the soft passenger seat.

It felt crazy. Wow. I didn't think it would feel like this.

We pulled away.

I dragged the seat belt across me, something I hadn't done for ten months.

Her speed increased.

My heart began to beat that one beat faster.

My mind kept telling me:

Say something ...
Slow down ...

I'm feeling sick ...
Anything ...

We approached the dual carriageway, cars going at all speeds, big lorries swaying.

I kept on smiling, answering Marianne's questions.

Then we were there at last, stopped at the side of the pavement.

"Here we are, love. That's the place you'll be working."

I saw a long, rough-looking building. No windows, as they were all bricked up.

I was still nervous.

I felt a little ill. Headache. Stomach empty.

"Oh, there's Dave now, that's who'll you'll be working with. He's the manager."

The worry came closer to me. There stood a white man in a long, black suede coat with a black hood covering his head.

He walked across with a young boy's walk.

"You're Tom then," he said, as I got out of the car.

"Yes. How are you?"

"I'm alright, mate. Come on then," Dave said in his rough-toned voice.

We walked through a white wooden door with gold-coloured handles.

I was stood looking down a long, dark hall filled with game-tables, old TVs and computer monitors.

Dave showed me around.

I started to feel a little better.

"Don't look so nervous," he said, and laughed.

First room: mirrored walls, bright yellow ceiling, a light wooden floor with plastic chairs against the wall.

"That's our dance room," he said

Second room: dark blue. It felt cosy. A few chairs, a long snooker table next to a small pool table. Nice smooth carpet.

I followed him around these nice warm colourful rooms with a single thought in my mind: I wouldn't mind owning a place like this.

I *could* own a place like this.

The smell of fresh-baked Welsh cakes was floating in the air and streaming into my nose. My stomach started to crave food.

I stepped into the fresh air again. I felt different. Normally doors would be opened for me. Officers would be around, keys would be ringing.

It felt so great. I felt free as a bird in the strong-blowing winds.

I started at a slow pace towards the local shop at the bottom of the hill. All the things I hadn't seen in months. Buses passed me, then a big fire engine with its loud, rough engine. I heard little screaming voices, children playing in their school playground.

I walked into the shop, looked around. I didn't know what to do, where to look. I wanted everything. I only had a small amount of money but wanted all the things I hadn't had for months.

I opened the fridge.

Wow, what a feeling! I hadn't opened a fridge in a long time. I hadn't opened a can for a while.

I went to the counter. Chewing gum, all different packets, blue, red, white. Something I wasn't allowed inside.

I gave them to the man who stood behind the till. I didn't care what pack, I just wanted to chew.